CW01521806

C O N T E N T S

The 'green planet'

Plants are all around us, and they make the world green. Only the ice caps, mountain tops and the most barren deserts have no plants – here it is too cold or too dry for them to grow.

Plants provide food for most living things. They do not need to eat because they make their own food – sugar, a carbohydrate – inside their leaves. There is a special substance inside their leaves that uses sunlight to provide the energy for making sugar. That substance is called **chlorophyll**. And guess what colour chlorophyll is? That's right – green!

Flowering plants These are the most advanced and successful group of plants. They come in many sizes and shapes. Sometimes the flowers are not very large or colourful, as with the grasses and many trees.

Conifers Pine trees, fir trees, cypresses and redwoods are called conifers because they produce *cones*. Conifers are much less varied than flowering plants – they are all either trees or bushes.

Algae Algae are very simple, primitive plants, compared to all the others shown here. They have no roots, although some seaweeds have a structure that can hold on to rocks, called a *holdfast*. Algae can grow only in water.

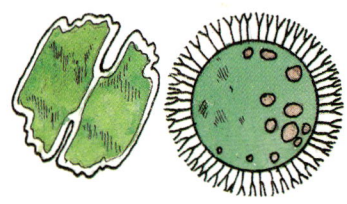

Mosses Some of the simplest plants to grow on land are the mosses. They do not have flowers, or proper roots. They have no waxy layer to protect their leaves and stop them from drying out. So most of them have to live in damp places.

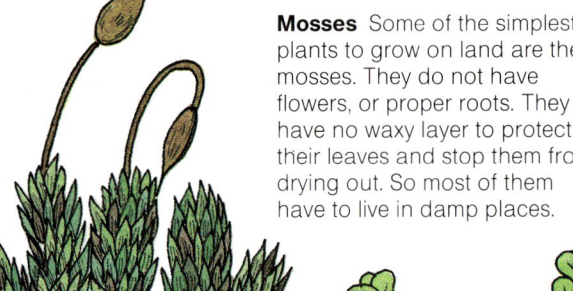

Seaweeds and **waterweeds** These are the largest of the algae. They grow along the shoreline, and in ponds, lakes and rivers. Like all plants, they need sunlight, and so cannot grow in deep water.

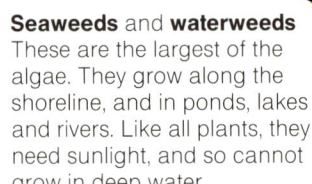

Liverworts Liverworts are related to mosses, but they look quite different because they have a flat, tongue-shaped body called a *thallus*. Like mosses, they are simple plants, and need damp places.

Ferns Ferns are fairly primitive plants which do not have flowers or seeds. Instead they produce tiny particles called *spores*. These spores are so small that they look like brown dust. Ferns are tougher than mosses, and grow taller because they have woody stems.

Horsetails These are primitive plants related to the ferns. You may see them growing by a river or as a weed in damp gardens.

Trees A tree is just a plant that grows very tall and has a single stem (called the *trunk*). Several different groups of plants have species which have developed into trees. These include the flowering plants, the conifers and the ferns.

Flowers and cones

Flowers These produce *pollen* and *egg cells*. The pollen may be blown by the wind from plant to plant, or carried by animals, usually insects. Pollen *fertilizes* the egg cell to produce a seed, which can then grow into a new plant.

Cones Cones may not look much like flowers, but they do the same job as the flowers of flowering plants. Inside them are pollen and egg cells. The pollen is blown from one tree to another by the wind. When pollen fertilizes the egg cells inside a cone, they develop into seeds.

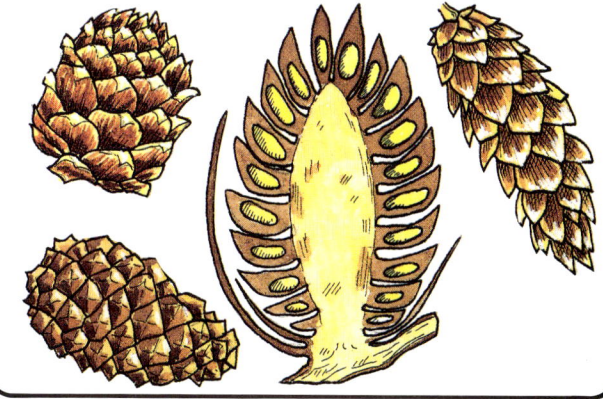

The smallest plants

As well as many different varieties of seaweed, the oceans also have plants which are very small and cannot be seen without a microscope. These tiny plants consist of just one cell – whereas a **dandelion** or a **rose bush** is made up of millions of cells. Microscopic plants float at the surface of the water and soak up the sunlight. They are found in lakes and ponds as well as in the sea. Most of these single cells belong to the group known as **algae**. The first plants lived in the seas and were similar to the microscopic algae that still exist today. In time, larger plants evolved. Eventually they moved out of the water onto land. The first plants to live on land were very like the modern mosses and liverworts.

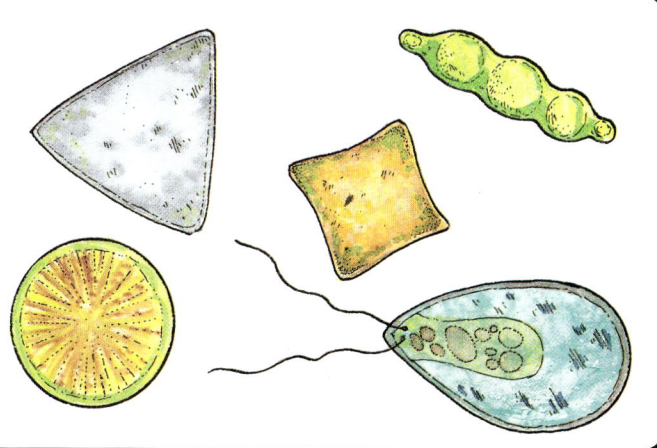

Is it a plant?

Most plants are green. Plants that do not contain chlorophyll are white or yellow. This happens very rarely in nature, but many garden plants and house plants have been produced with white patches or stripes on their leaves. They are known as **variegated** leaves.

Sometimes plants have other colours or **pigments** in their leaves, which mask the green chlorophyll. Some kinds of seaweeds use brown, red, or purple pigments to help them absorb light that has filtered through water.

There are also some land plants that have coloured pigments in their leaves. These are often used in gardens and houses as an alternative to decorative green **foliage** (leaves).

Find the plants

Look carefully at the eight pictures below. Only four of them are plants. **Which ones do you think they are?**

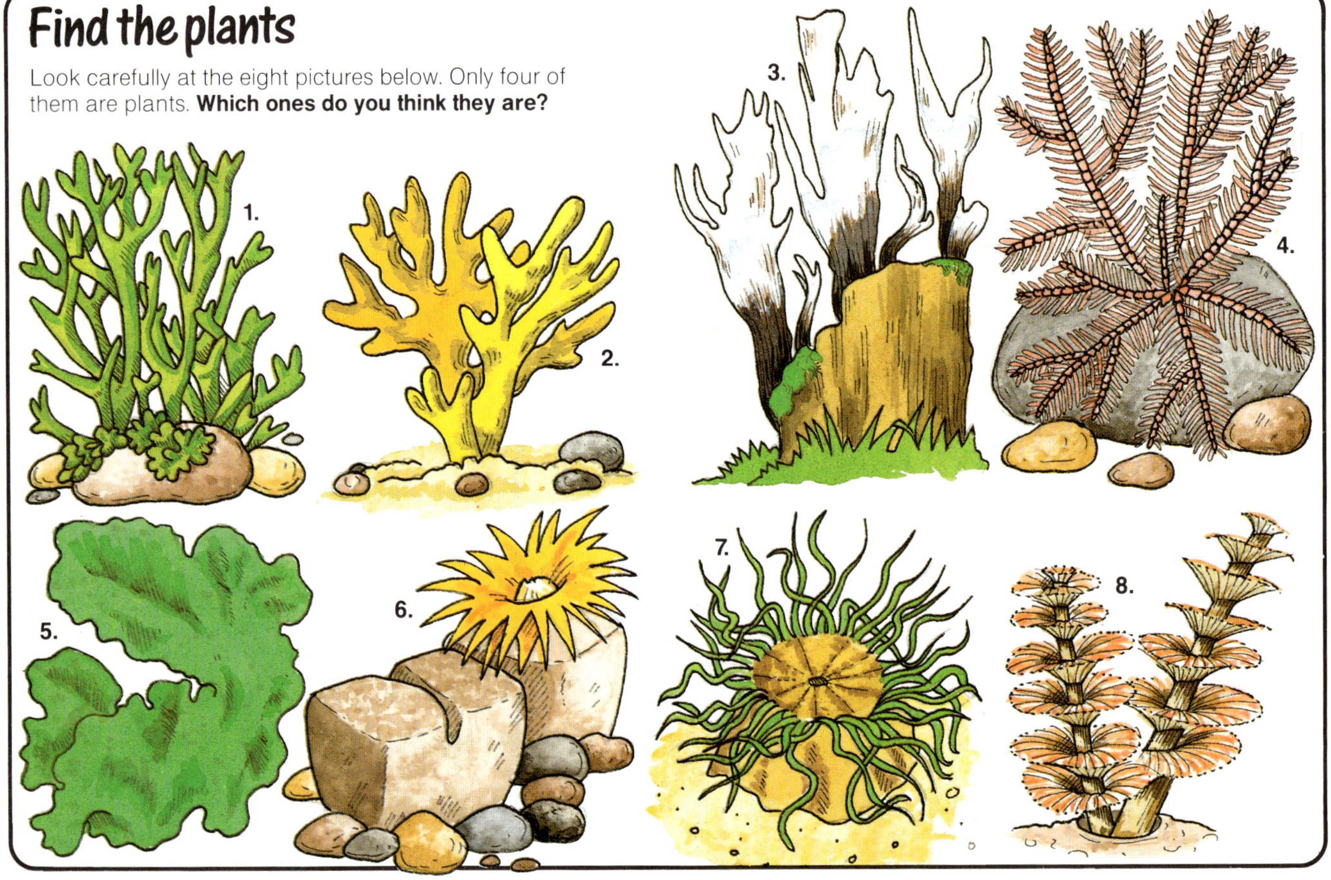

1.

2.

3.

4.

5.

6.

7.

8.

STAYING PUT

Plants make their own food, so, unlike animals, they don't have to move around looking for it. So all plants, except the microscopic algae, stay in one place. For land plants, this has its advantages. They can push their roots down into the ground to get water, and roots help to anchor them when the wind blows. Being in one place also means that plants can spread out or up, and keep on growing as long as the conditions are right.

LAZY ANIMALS

Some animals also stay in one place. It is easy to mistake these for plants. Animals that live like this can be seen in the sea where they feed on tiny particles of food in the water. Among them are **fanworms**, **sponges** and **corals**.

Fanworms

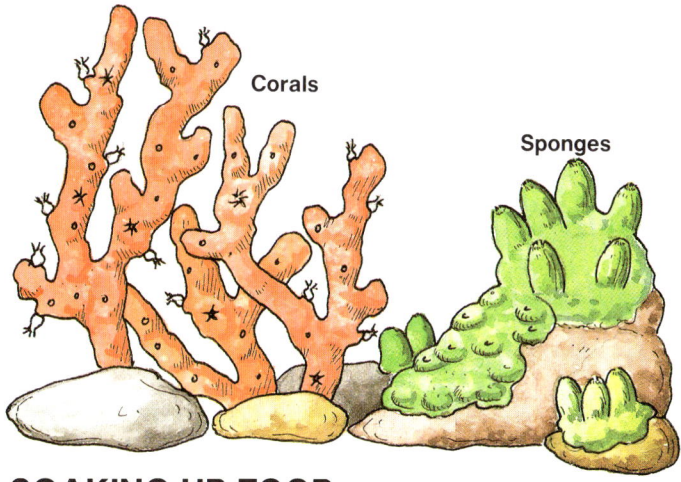

Corals

Sponges

SOAKING UP FOOD

Mushrooms and toadstools belong to a group called the **fungi**. They are neither plants nor animals, but because they stay in one place they are sometimes mistaken for plants. Fungi cannot make their own food. They grow over dead wood pushing long threads called *hyphae* deep into the wood to soak up food. Some grow on living trees. Plants or animals that do this are known as *parasites*.

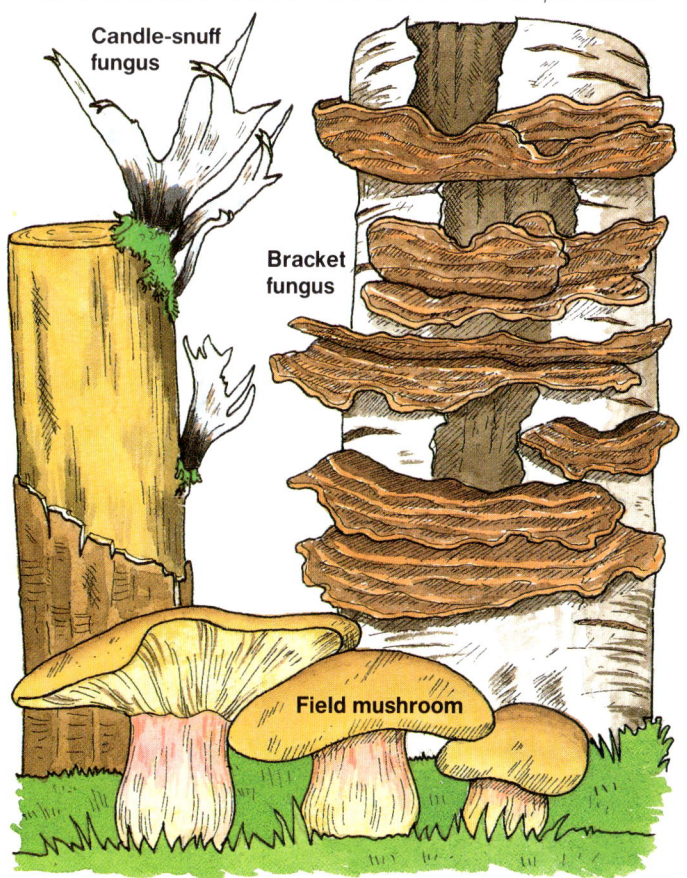

Candle-snuff fungus

Bracket fungus

Field mushroom

Inside a plant

A plant such as a **shepherd's-purse** has roots, stems and leaves. The roots absorb water from the soil. They also take up chemicals, called **nutrients**, that the plant needs to grow.

The water and nutrients travel up through the roots and stems, inside narrow tubes. They eventually reach the leaves, where the plant's food is made. The plant must have water and nutrients in order to make its food.

The food produced by the leaves goes to all the other parts of the plant. It travels back down the stem to the roots, which cannot make their own food because they are in the soil and get no sunlight.

WHAT IS EVAPORATION?

When you hang a wet towel on the washing line, the warmth of the sun turns the water into a gas. Eventually the towel is dry. This is called *evaporation*. Most leaves are rather like wet towels except that they have a waxy, waterproof layer on the outside to keep the water in.

The leaves of the **eucalyptus** have a thick, waxy layer that makes the leaves look bluish-green.

HOLES IN THE LEAVES

Plants have a difficult problem to solve. To make food from sunlight they need a gas, called *carbon dioxide*. They combine this gas with water to make sugar.

Carbon dioxide is in the air around us and it gets into the leaves of plants through holes called *stomata*.

The problem is that water can get out of the stomata as easily as air can get in. So the leaves are in danger of drying out. Plants solve the problem by only opening for as long as they really need to. Only in very dry weather do plants lose more water than they can replace from the soil.

Eucalyptus leaf

Holly leaf

The thick, waxy layer of the **holly** leaf makes it look glossy.

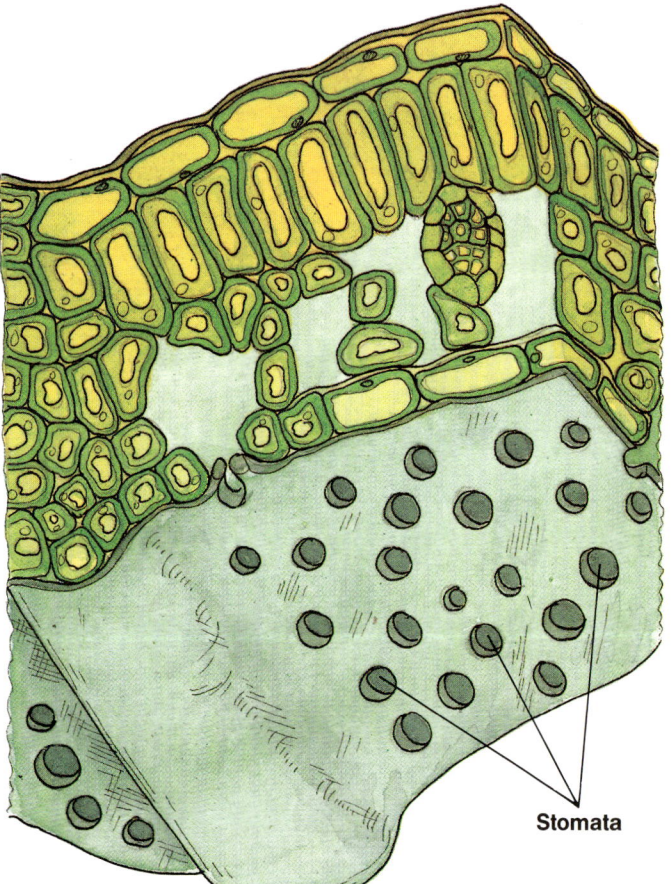

Stomata

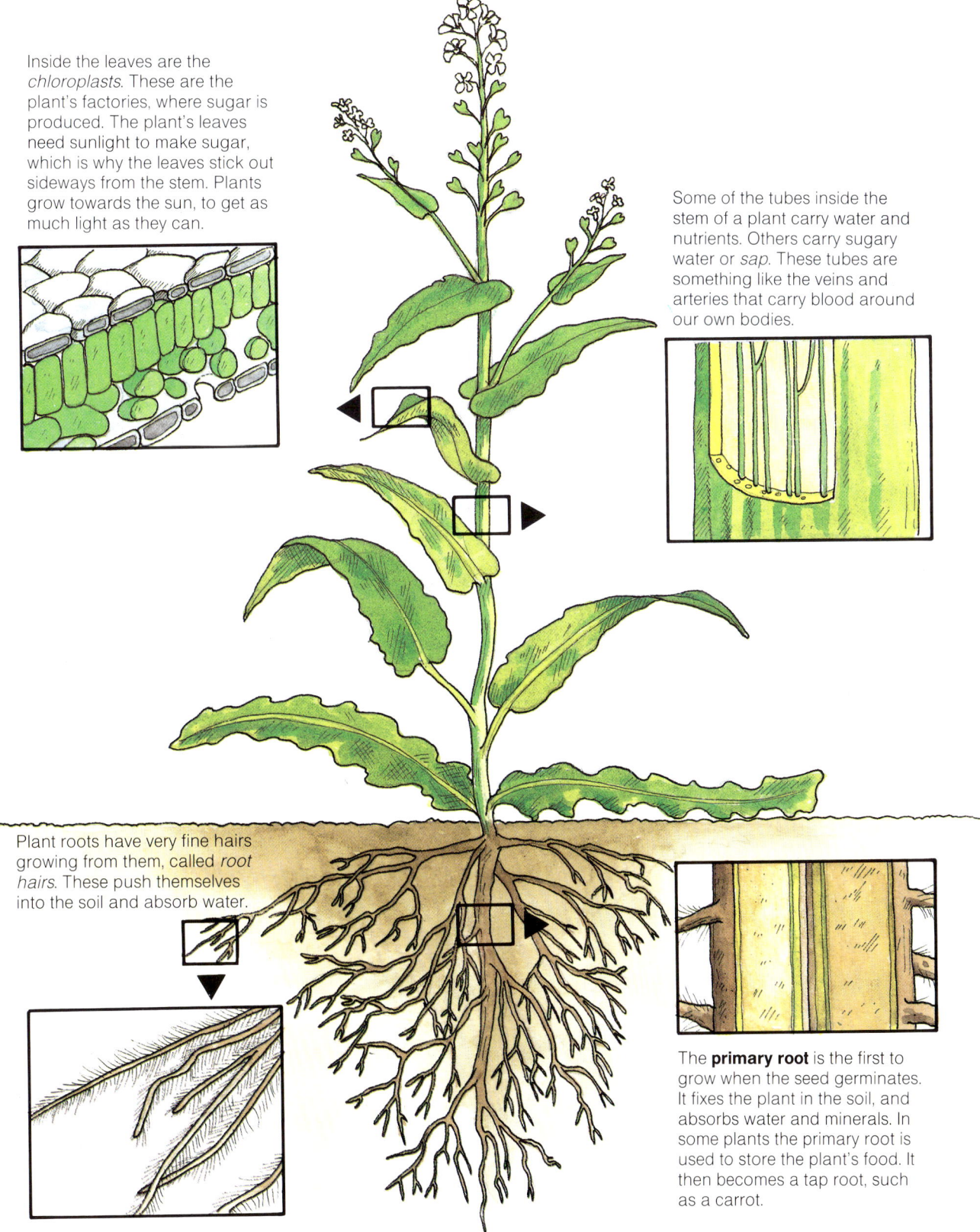

Inside the leaves are the *chloroplasts*. These are the plant's factories, where sugar is produced. The plant's leaves need sunlight to make sugar, which is why the leaves stick out sideways from the stem. Plants grow towards the sun, to get as much light as they can.

Some of the tubes inside the stem of a plant carry water and nutrients. Others carry sugary water or *sap*. These tubes are something like the veins and arteries that carry blood around our own bodies.

Plant roots have very fine hairs growing from them, called *root hairs*. These push themselves into the soil and absorb water.

The **primary root** is the first to grow when the seed germinates. It fixes the plant in the soil, and absorbs water and minerals. In some plants the primary root is used to store the plant's food. It then becomes a tap root, such as a carrot.

Plants everywhere

*Plants can live in many different places. Some of these places have heavy rainfall, others are very dry. Some are bitterly cold, others very windy or extremely hot. Through the slow process of **evolution**, plants have gradually changed, so that they can cope with these difficult climates.*

AS DRY AS A DESERT

The problem in the desert is not that there's no water. It's that it all comes at once in a sudden downpour. So what many desert plants do is to save water for a not-so-rainy day. The cacti store water in their fat stems. They have spines instead of leaves, because leaves are thin and lose a lot of moisture when the sun shines on them. The spines lose less water and they help to keep thirsty animals away.

LONG SNOWY WINTERS

The cold lands of the north have very long winters, with plenty of snow. The conifers that grow here are well suited to this climate. They do not lose their leaves in winter, so they can start making food as soon as the spring arrives. Their leaves, which are long, tough, wax-coated needles, survive very cold, dry conditions without being damaged. And the branches of the trees slope downwards, so that they shed snow easily.

TOWERING TREES

In the rainforest, the climate is very good for plants – plenty of rain and warmth all year round. For millions of years there has been a silent battle for sunlight going on between these trees. The tallest ones get the light and put others in the shade. Through the slow changes of evolution, some have become extraordinarily tall – 45 metres or more.

Where do they live?

Look at the leaves of each of these plants. **Where do you think they live? Try to match them to the five habitats.**

Choose from these habitats:
desert, pond, rainforest, stream, rocky crevices near the sea

1.

2.

3.

4.

5.

Food chains

Animals live by eating plants, or by eating other animals that live on plants. One way, or another, all living things need plants. They are the beginning of what are called **food chains**. In oceans, the food chains begin with plants that are very small and cannot be seen without a microscope. These are then eaten by microscopic animals. Together, these plants and animals are known as **plankton** and they float at the surface of the sea.

On land, food chains begin with plants such as grasses. These are then eaten by insects, birds and animals.

Going green

If you take some water from a pond it looks quite clear, but leave it on a sunny windowsill for a week or two and it turns bright green. **What do you think has happened?** If some **pond snails** are put into the jam jar, the water soon becomes clear again. **What do you think snails eat?**

Make your own food chain

Can you make a food chain from the pond animals shown below? Trace them onto a piece of paper and colour them in. Now cut them out and try to arrange them into two food chains. If you stick them onto a blank piece of paper, you can draw arrows between them to show who eats what.

Food chains such as this do not tell the whole story. Most animals have many different sources of food – not just one.

(answer – page 37)

Algae

Hobby

Tadpole

Adult dragonfly

Fox

Waterweed

Mallard

OUT IN THE OCEAN

We can show which animals eat other animals, and which ones eat plants, by arranging them in a *food chain*. This is one ocean food chain. If you look closely at it, you will see that the **killer whale** needs the tiny plants floating at the ocean's surface. Even though it cannot see them, they are the source of all its food!

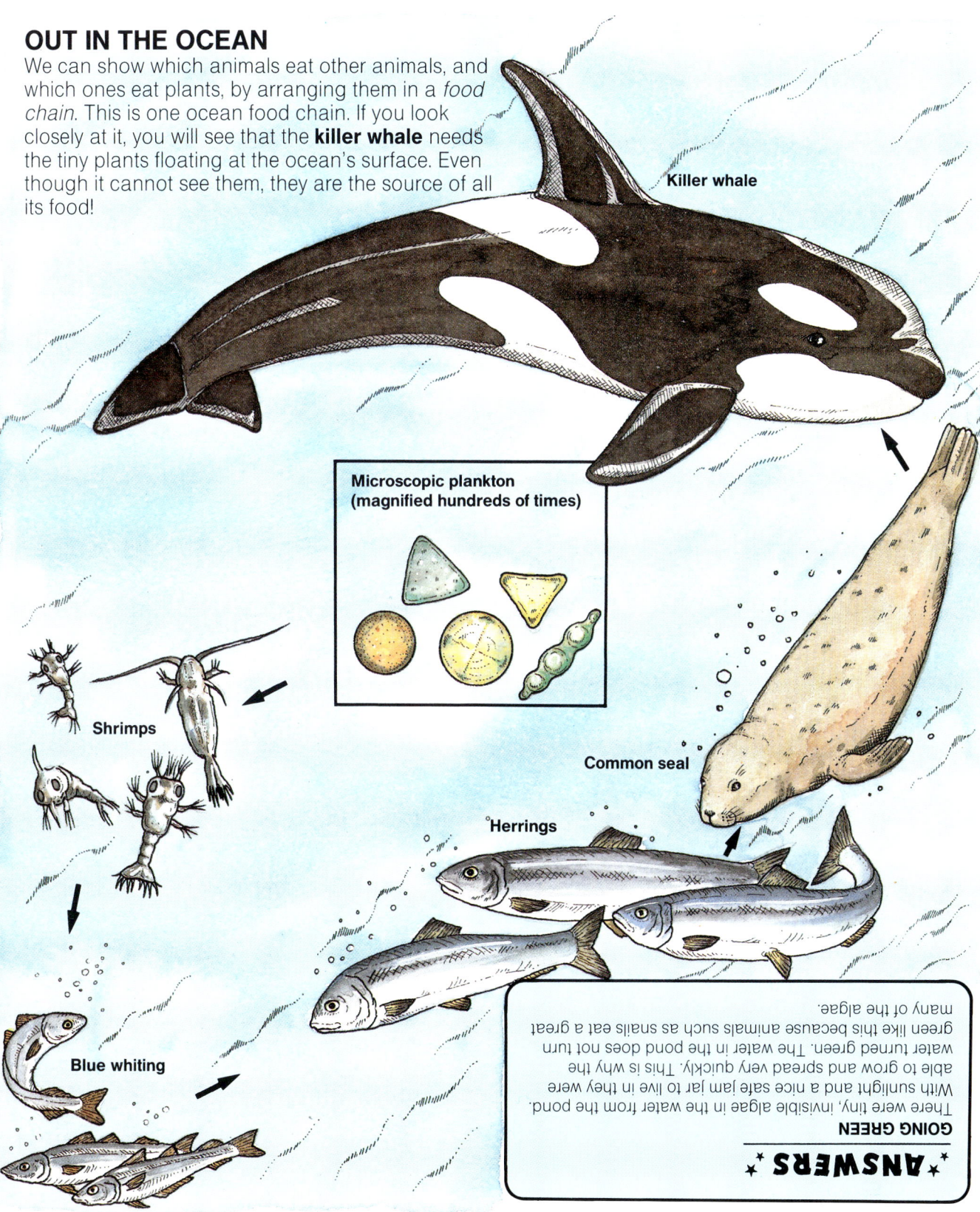

Killer whale

**Microscopic plankton
(magnified hundreds of times)**

Shrimps

Common seal

Herrings

Blue whiting

★ ANSWERS ★

GOING GREEN
There were tiny, invisible algae in the water from the pond. With sunlight and a nice safe jam jar to live in they were able to grow and spread very quickly. This is why the water turned green. The water in the pond does not turn green like this because animals such as snails eat a great many of the algae.

15

Going round in cycles

All living things must have food to grow. They use this food to make up their body tissues and to provide them with energy. The basic ingredients of this food are carbon, oxygen, nitrogen and hydrogen. These are all around us – in the air and in the soil. But animals cannot use them as they are, only plants, and some

bacteria, can do this. Plants make their own food from these ingredients in the process known as photosynthesis (see pages 10 and 11). Some animals obtain their food by eating plants, others by eating plant-eating animals. In this way, we can see that all living creatures depend on plants for their survival.

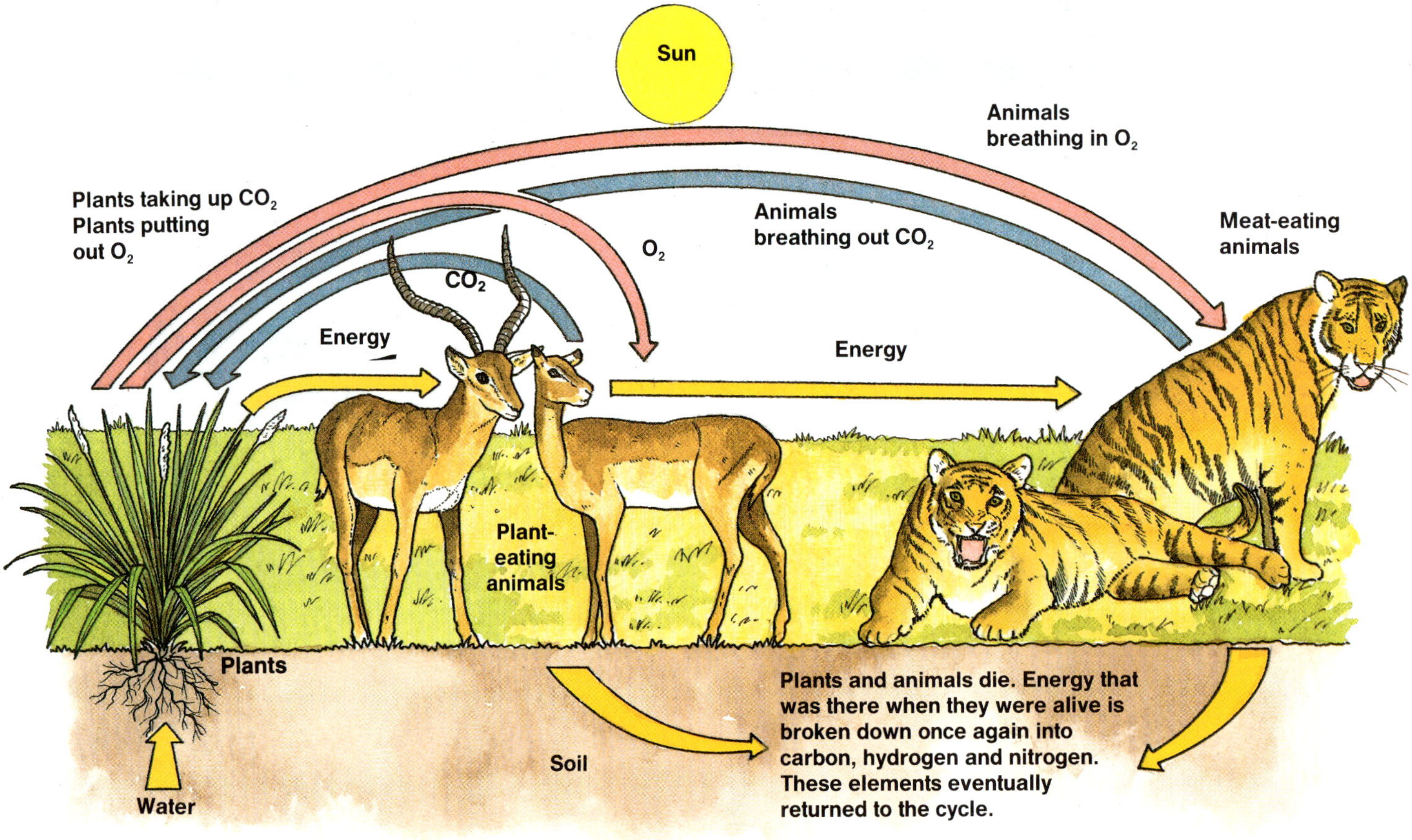

Sun

Animals breathing in O_2

Plants taking up CO_2
Plants putting out O_2

Animals breathing out CO_2

Meat-eating animals

CO_2

O_2

Energy

Energy

Plant-eating animals

Plants

Soil

Water

Plants and animals die. Energy that was there when they were alive is broken down once again into carbon, hydrogen and nitrogen. These elements eventually returned to the cycle.

THE CARBON CYCLE

Carbon is found in the atmosphere in the form of a gas called carbon dioxide (CO_2). Plants absorb this CO_2 in the sunlight and join it with water to make carbohydrates which provide energy. This forms the tissues of the plant. When an animal eats a plant, the carbohydrates are broken down once again into CO_2, water and energy. The CO_2 is released back into the atmosphere when the animal breathes. Plants are essential food for animals and balance the levels of CO_2 and oxygen (O_2) in the air, thus allowing animals to breathe.

THE OXYGEN CYCLE

The oxygen cycle works in the opposite way to the carbon cycle. When plants photosynthesize, they put oxygen into the atmosphere as a waste product. Animals need this oxygen in order to get energy from the food they eat. They take in oxygen by breathing.

The carbon and oxygen cycles also take place in ponds, rivers and seas. They occur in much the same way except that the gasses are dissolved in the water. Without plants, there would not be any oxygen for animals to breathe.

NITROGEN CYCLE

Nitrogen is also important to plants and animals, because they use it to form their body tissues. It is only made available to living things by nitrogen-fixing bacteria in the soil and in the root nodules of plants such as peas and beans. These convert nitrogen from the air into a chemical that plants can absorb. The nitrogen is then passed on to animals in the plants they eat. Eventually all plants and animals die, and the nitrogen is returned to the soil.

⋆*ANSWERS*⋆

PLAYING WITH PONDWEED
The pondweed was giving off oxygen. Most plants do this; the oxygen is a product of photosynthesis. A flame will burn stronger when there is oxygen about. When the splint was held into the jar it glowed more brightly. This proves that the plant was giving off oxygen.

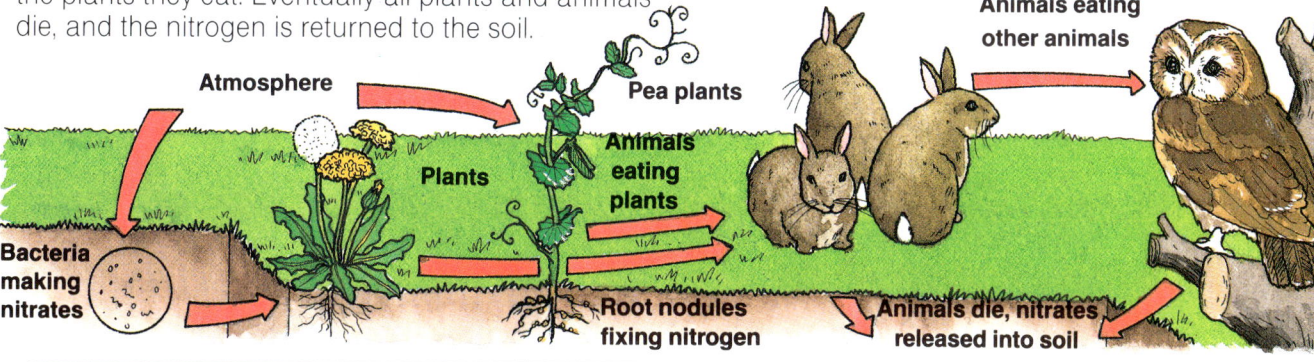

Atmosphere

Pea plants

Animals eating other animals

Plants

Animals eating plants

Bacteria making nitrates

Root nodules fixing nitrogen

Animals die, nitrates released into soil

Playing with pondweed

We can use this experiment to show part of one of the cycles described on these pages. You will need some water, a bowl, a small jar, a funnel, some pondweed, a box of matches and a wood splint.

1. Fill the bowl with water and put the pondweed in the bottom. Rest your funnel upside down over the top of the pondweed.

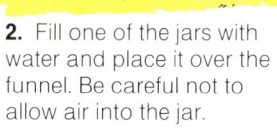

2. Fill one of the jars with water and place it over the funnel. Be careful not to allow air into the jar.

3. Place your bowl in the sunlight or under a bright light for a week. Bubbles of gas should rise from the pondweed and collect in the jar.

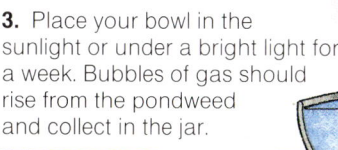

4. After a week remove the jar from the funnel and put an airtight lid on it. Keep the mouth of the jar under the water and do not allow any of the gas to escape.

5. Light the wood splint and blow out the flame so that the wood is glowing. Quickly remove the lid of your jar and put the splint into it. The splint will glow more brightly or burst into flame. It does this in the presence of a certain gas. What gas do you think the pondweed has been giving off?

If nothing happens, try again. It may be that you lost some of the gas from the jar before putting on the lid.

How plants grow

Plants need sunlight, water and warmth in order to grow. If you look at a houseplant on a windowsill, you will see that it is growing towards the window. What happens is that the tip of the stem produces chemicals called **hormones**, which work their way back down the stem and that tells it how fast to grow. On the side furthest from the light, the stem grows faster than on the side nearest the light. Because of this, the stem begins to bend – in the direction of the light.

Plants also have to make sure that they flower and set seed at the right time. In spring, they wait until it gets warm before they start growing. And the length of the days tells them when it is time to flower.

WAITING FOR THE RAINS

Some desert plants, like cacti, survive by storing water. Others make the most of the rains which, when they do come, are usually heavy and short. These plants spend most of the year as seeds, lying quietly in the desert sand or soil. Then, when it rains, they rush into action. In a few days the seeds can come to life, or *germinate*, and the plants grow to their full size. In another day or two, they have produced their flowers and set seed. By the time the desert is beginning to dry out again, their seeds are ripe, and ready to fall to the ground. There they must wait, for months or even years, until the rain falls again.

SEED SURVIVAL

Seeds that fall onto cold, damp ground, have a thick skin which helps keep out the bacteria and fungi that can cause them to rot. Thanks to this skin, they can live through a cold winter and start growing in the spring.

For some plants, this is the only way they can survive the winter – the plant itself dies. These are called *annuals*. Other plants, called *perennials*, survive the winter, although they usually produce seeds as well.

There are also plants called *biennials*, that live for just two years. In the first year they build up a fat, juicy tap root. In the second year they use the food in the tap root to help them grow and flower. Once they have set seed they die.

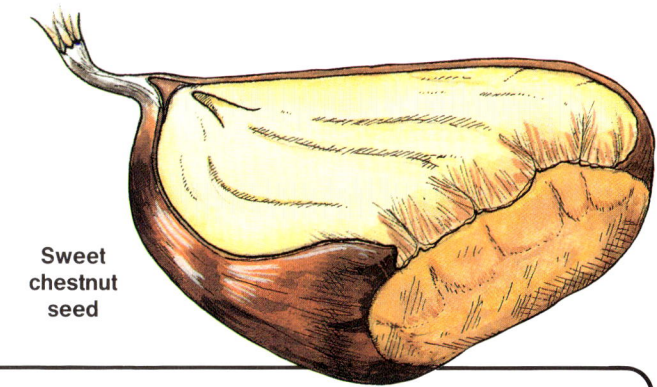

Sweet chestnut seed

THE FORCE OF GRAVITY

Seeds that grow in the dark, in the soil or under leaves, still send their shoots up and their roots down. In this case, the plant hormones are not responding to the light, but to the force of gravity.

How do they survive the winter?

Look at a flower bed or vegetable garden in winter. Where have all the plants gone? Even if the gardener does not put in any new plants or seeds the next spring, something will come up. You will see many of the same plants that were there last summer. **So how did they survive the winter?** If you look carefully at this picture you will see some clues.

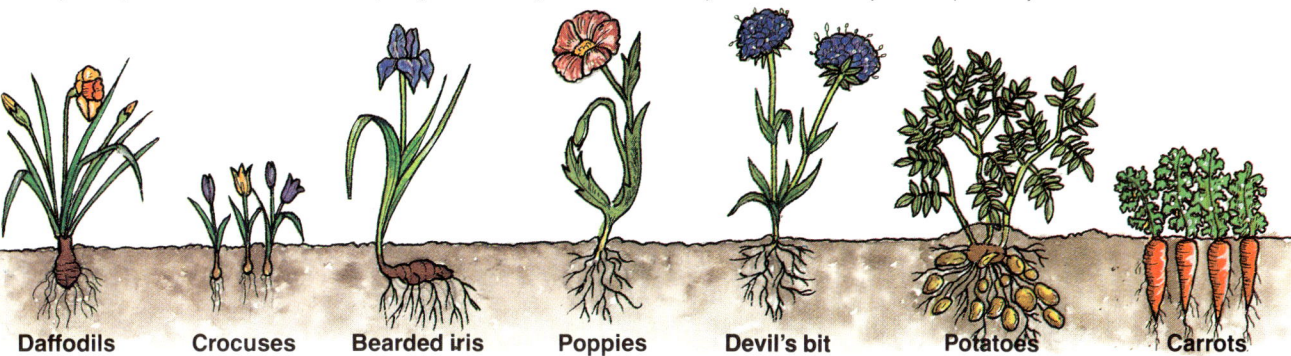

Daffodils   **Crocuses**   **Bearded iris**   **Poppies**   **Devil's bit**   **Potatoes**   **Carrots**

Bursting into bloom

The coloured petals and sweet scents of flowers are attractive not only to us, but also to other, much smaller animals. These animals carry pollen from one flower to another and are called **pollinators***. The pollen joins with an egg cell, deep inside the flower, and a seed begins to form.*

GONE WITH THE WIND

Some plants use the wind to carry their pollen from flower to flower. Grasses do this, and so do most trees. *Catkins* are often seen on wind-pollinated trees. When the wind blows, the catkins dance about and this sends the pollen flying off into the air. Because they use the wind, these flowers do not need to attract pollinators with bright colours or wonderful scents.

Most pollen is carried by insects such as bees, hoverflies and moths. In tropical countries, there are some birds and bats that do the same thing. In most cases, the flowers produce a syrup called **nectar** *for the pollinator to eat. It is as if they are 'paying' the insect, bird or bat, to carry the pollen for them.*

Plants that lure bats have a musky scent. Most are white or cream to show up well in the dark.

Nectar-eating bat

For pollinators that fly at night, scents are very important. Flowers that attract moths have a sweet scent.

Night-flying moth

Summer sneezes

Do you sneeze the summer away? If you do, then you are probably one of the unlucky people who have hay fever. The cause of your trouble is pollen, but not the pollen from roses and other garden flowers. It is the pollen from wind-pollinated plants that makes you sneeze because this is produced in huge quantities and goes swirling about in the air. People with hay fever have an *allergy* to certain kinds of pollen, which means that their bodies react to it as if it were harmful.

Most bird-pollinated flowers are brightly-coloured. Birds have little sense of smell, so these flowers are unscented.

Sword-billed hummingbird

Butterflies can see reds very well.

Spot the pollinator

Flowers need to be just right to attract the best kind of pollinator. **Can you match these flowers up with their pollinators?**

Honeysuckle releases its sweet scent at night.

The **cup and saucer vine's** large flowers give off a musky smell at night.

Brugmansia saiguinea has its nectar near the base of the flower, where it is joined to the plant.

★ **ANSWERS** ★

SPOT THE POLLINATOR

The **cup and saucer vine** is pollinated by bats. Notice how large the flowers are – a bat needs more to eat than an insect!

Brugmansia saiguinea is pollinated by the **sword-billed hummingbird** – no other animal could reach that far!

Honeysuckle is pollinated by night-flying moths with long mouthparts that can reach deep into its tubular flowers.

Setting seed

A seed is a plant's way of making new plants. But it is no good if the young plants grow right next to their parents. Then they would be competing with their parents for light and water. As plants are rooted in one place, they have to **disperse***, or spread, their seed so that the young plants grow far away. They have evolved many different ways of doing this.*

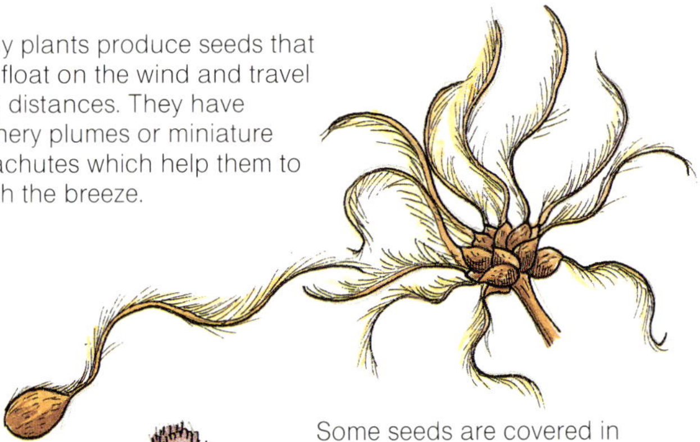

Some plants wrap their seeds up in juicy fruits. Birds eat the fruit and carry the seeds away. Because the seed has a tough coat it passes through the bird's gut without being damaged. It falls to the ground with the bird's droppings, and there it can germinate and grow.

Many plants produce seeds that can float on the wind and travel long distances. They have feathery plumes or miniature parachutes which help them to catch the breeze.

Some seeds are covered in hooks, which catch on animals' fur or people's clothing. Later they are brushed off, many miles away. Seeds of this type are often called *burs*.

Spreading their seeds

Here are some plants that have special ways of dispersing their seeds. **Can you guess what they are?**

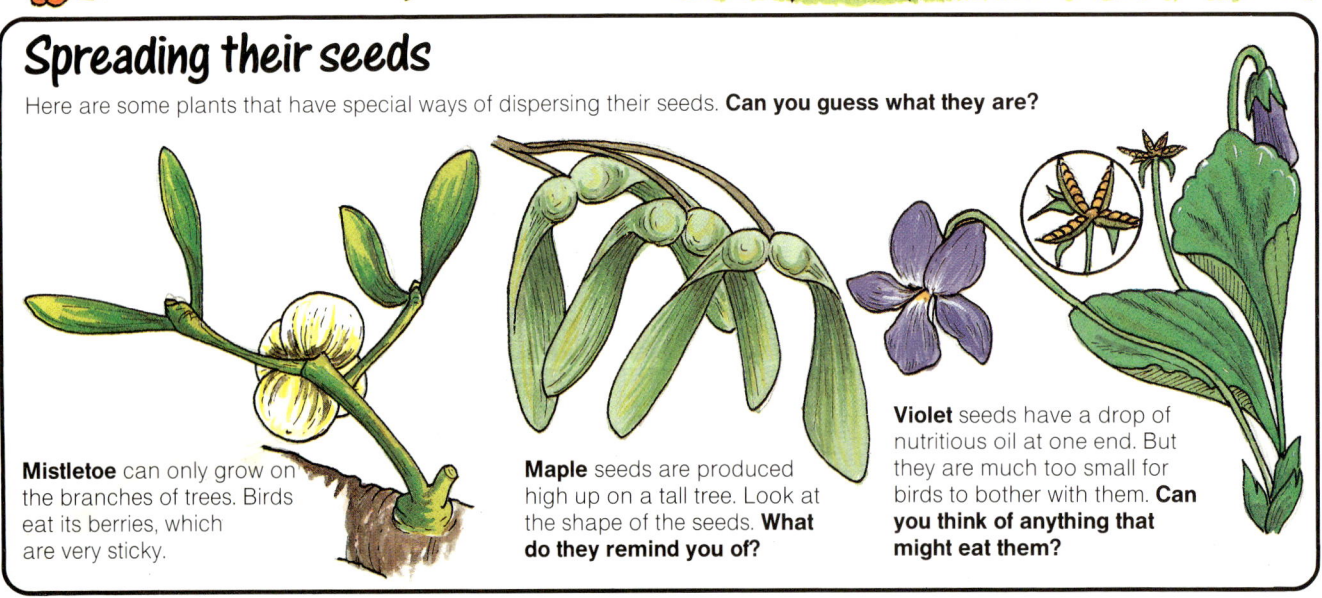

Mistletoe can only grow on the branches of trees. Birds eat its berries, which are very sticky.

Maple seeds are produced high up on a tall tree. Look at the shape of the seeds. **What do they remind you of?**

Violet seeds have a drop of nutritious oil at one end. But they are much too small for birds to bother with them. **Can you think of anything that might eat them?**

Plants that grow near water often have oily seeds that float. They are carried downstream by the water and washed up onto a bank. This should be a good place to grow.

Nut-trees package their seeds inside nuts, which make good winter food. Squirrels often hide the nuts for the cold months ahead. If forgotten, these can grow into new trees.

✫ ANSWERS ✫

SPREADING THEIR SEEDS

When birds feed on **mistletoe** berries, a lot of sticky juice gets left on their beaks. To get their beaks clean, they wipe them on the branches of trees. Some seeds get wiped onto the branch as well.

The two 'arms' of the **maple seed** are rather like the propellor on an early aeroplane. They make the seed whirl around and around as it falls, and this helps it to travel on the breeze away from the parent tree.

Violet seeds are carried off by ants, who use the oil to feed the young ones in their nests. The rest of the seed is left, and can grow into a new plant.

Some plants produce seeds in pods, which snap open when dry and shoot their seeds in all directions.

Plants without seeds

Only flowering plants and conifers produce seeds. All other plants produce spores instead. These are often so small that you cannot see them. But you can see the brown dust on the underside of fern leaves – this contains millions of spores. Because spores are so tiny they are carried a long way by the wind.

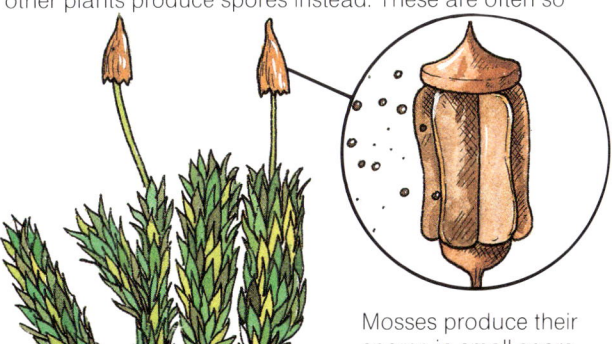

Mosses produce their spores in small spore capsules, which grow up from the plants on stalks.

Ferns produce their spores underneath their leaves, in clusters known as *sori*.

New plants from old

Plants have many different ways of spreading themselves, apart from producing seeds. They can make new plants grow from their roots, tubers or stems – even from bits of leaves. This is known as **vegetative reproduction**. It is also called **asexual reproduction** because there is no joining of pollen cells and egg cells as there is when seeds are produced. As a result, the young plants are exactly the same as their parents.

RUNNING ALONG

Plants can send stems out sideways, as grasses do. When the stems reach a certain length they grow new roots. Some plants produce special extra-long stems to get the young plant even further away from them. These long stems are called *stolons* or *runners*. You can see them on **strawberry** plants, **mint** plants and the house plants known as **spider plants**. If you grow mint in the garden it soon becomes a pest, growing everywhere.

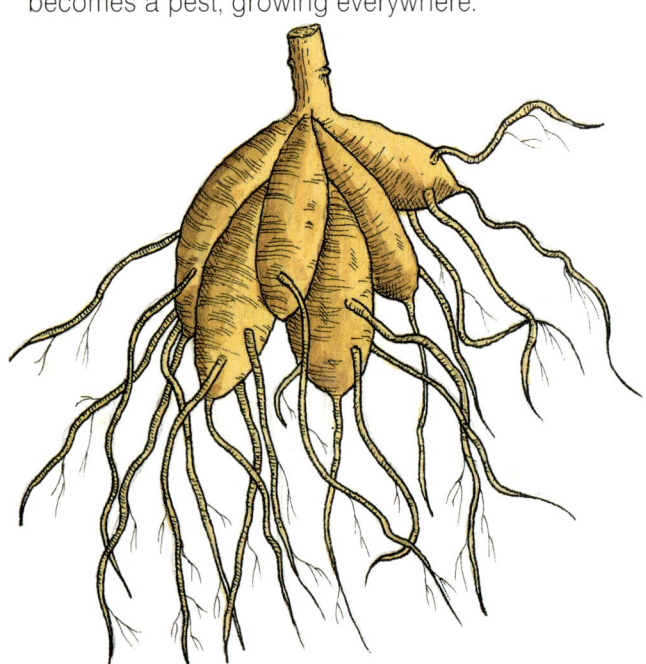

TUBERS

Tubers, rhizomes and bulbs (see page 19) can all help a plant to reproduce, as well as getting it through the winter. If you look closely at a potato, you will see that it has many 'eyes'. Each one of these could grow into a new potato plant. A **dahlia** tuber (left) also has many parts, and a gardener will split it to get several new dahlia plants.

GROWING FROM TWIGS

Willow trees grow near water and their twigs snap off easily. If a fallen twig is carried downstream and becomes embedded in some mud, it will produce new roots from one end and leaves from the other. Eventually it grows into a new tree. Many other plants can produce new plants from tiny bits of themselves. Gardeners make use of this when they 'take cuttings' from plants such as **roses** and **geraniums**.

Taking cuttings

1. Get some clean glass jars and put 5 centimetres of water into each one.

2. Now cut off short lengths of stem from various plants. They should be about 10–15cm long.

3. Put them into the water and watch them for a week or two. Some of them, at least, should produce roots from the bottom of the stem.

4. When the cuttings have four of more good roots, you can plant them out in soil and watch them grow.

Plant protection

When animals are in danger they can run away or hide. But a plant is always rooted to the spot. So how does it defend itself against animals that want to eat it?

And what about animals with big feet who don't always look where they are going? Plants have to be quite tough if they are to survive.

STINGING NETTLES
Stinging nettles are actually covered with tiny 'needles' full of a poison that they inject into the skin. Animals soon learn not to try eating them.

PRICKLY PLANTS
In the desert, plants that store water have more than just food to offer animals. So it is no wonder that cacti and other desert plants are heavily defended with sharp spines.

LYING LOW
A lot of plants survive by keeping their leaves low to the ground. Some 'learn' to hug the ground if they are often eaten or cut. Look at the **dandelions** growing in a lawn and compare them with ones growing on wasteland or in hedgerows. The ones in the lawn produce their leaves and flowers on very short stalks because they are cut every time the lawn is mown. Dandelions that are not mown or nibbled can grow to heights of 30 cm or more.

Self defence

Here are some plants with unusual ways of keeping out of danger. **Can you think what they are?**

Lithops, or **stone plants**, can be grown as house plants, and you can see them quite clearly in the pot. But what about when they grow in the desert, which is where they come from?

This sensitive plant has delicate juicy leaves. If you touch them, they collapse and hang downwards, but they recover later.

Teasel plants have little basins where water can collect around the main stem.

*** ANSWERS ***

SELF DEFENCE
_____

Because the leaves of the **stone plants** look so much like real stones, animals that might eat them pass them by without a second look. This is known as *camouflage*. Animals like fresh juicy plants, not ones that have wilted. When a grazing animal such as a deer, touches the leaves

of the **Mimosa**, they collapse, and no longer look so appetizing. The sudden movement of the leaves probably startles the animal as well.

Ants would like to feed on the nectar of **teasel** flowers. But ants do not carry pollen from plant to plant as flying insects like butterflies do. The only way ants can reach the flowers is to climb the main stem, and the pools of water act as traps for these unwelcome insects.

POISONED FRUIT

All sorts of animals like to eat juicy fruits. But when it comes to dispersing the seeds (see page 22), birds do a better job than mice or other animals. This is because they fly from place to place – so they take the seeds further away. Plants have a better chance of survival if birds eat their fruits, but how can they keep mice and other furry animals away without putting birds off too? The answer, for plants such as **ivy**, is to produce poisons that affect mammals but not birds.

Woodland giants

A tree grows as tall as it can in order to get plenty of light. But a tall plant has to have a really thick, tough stem, or it would collapse. It is the strong stems or **trunks** *of trees that give us wood, one of the most useful and versatile materials on Earth.*

If you look at wood, you will see that it has a **grain***, and an expert can tell what type of tree it came from just by looking at the grain. But what exactly produces the grain? The tree produces it, and for very good reasons.*

HARDWOOD AND SOFTWOOD

There are two main types of trees – the flowering trees and the conifers. Wood from conifers is mostly easy to cut or nail through. Wood from flowering trees is usually much tougher. For this reason, the wood from conifers is called *softwood* and that from flowering trees is called *hardwood*. But these names are not really very good ones. Some conifers, such as the **pitch pine**, produce extremely hard wood. And it is a flowering tree that produces the softest wood of all – **balsa** wood.

AGING TREES

How can you tell the age of a tree? There is one way, but only if the tree has been chopped down!

As the tree grows, its trunk grows outwards, getting fatter every year. The new wood is added underneath the bark. Where there is a summer and winter season, trees do not grow at a steady rate. The trunk has a spurt of growth in spring, and then continues growing more slowly during the summer and autumn. This pattern of growth produces *tree rings* – one wide, soft ring, and one narrow, hard ring each year. So, by counting the rings on a tree that has been felled, you can tell how old it was.

TWO-WAY TRAFFIC

There is a constant two-way traffic in every tree trunk. Water from the roots travels up to the leaves through channels called *xylem*. Sap travels down from the leaves through channels called *phloem*. Other channels called *medullary rays* take the sap inwards, towards the centre of the trunk.

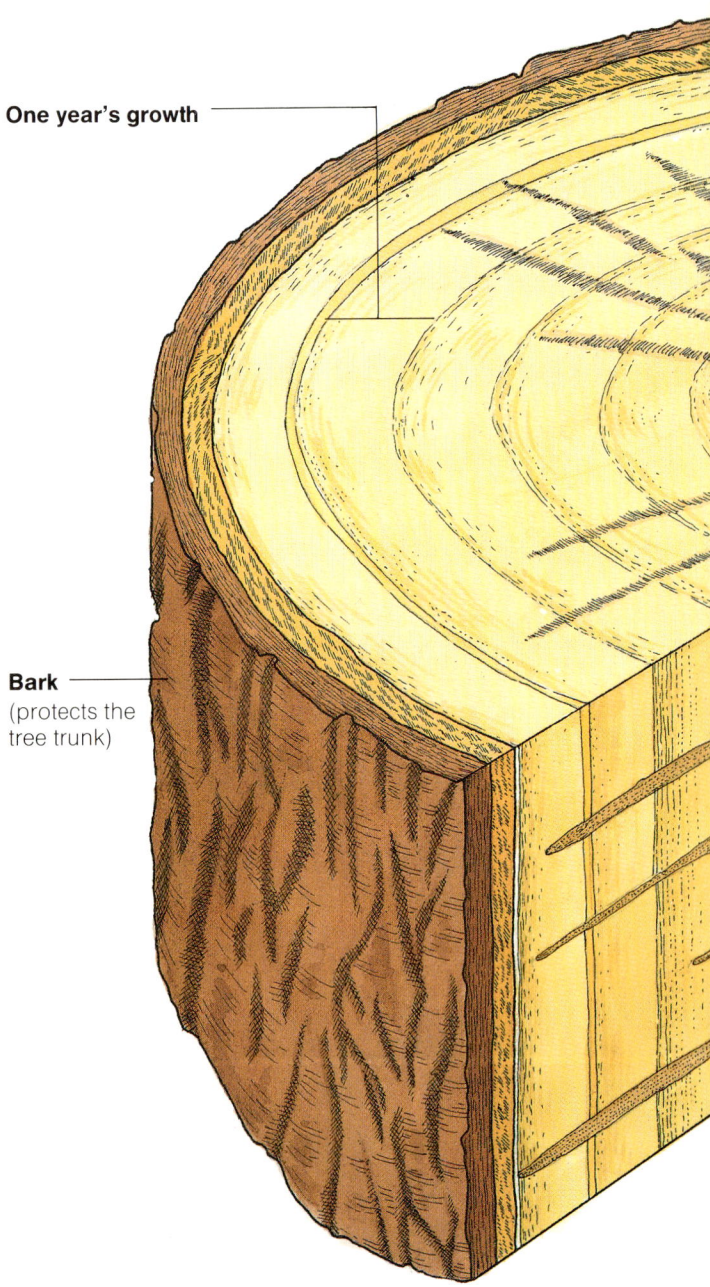

One year's growth

Bark
(protects the tree trunk)

HEARTWOOD AND SAPWOOD

Once a tree trunk reaches a certain thickness, the wood at the centre begins to die. This wood, known as *heartwood*, no longer conducts water. But it is still important to the tree as it helps to make the trunk stronger. The outer wood, which still conducts water, is called *sapwood*.

A KNOTTY PROBLEM

If you look at some wooden furniture, especially pine, you may see patterns of rings or *knots* in the surface. Do you know what causes them?

The branches of trees have xylem and phloem just like the trunk, and these channels connect up with the channels in the trunk. Where a branch goes off from the trunk of a tree, its channels penetrate deep into the trunk. When the trunk is cut up for wood, the branch shows as a knot.

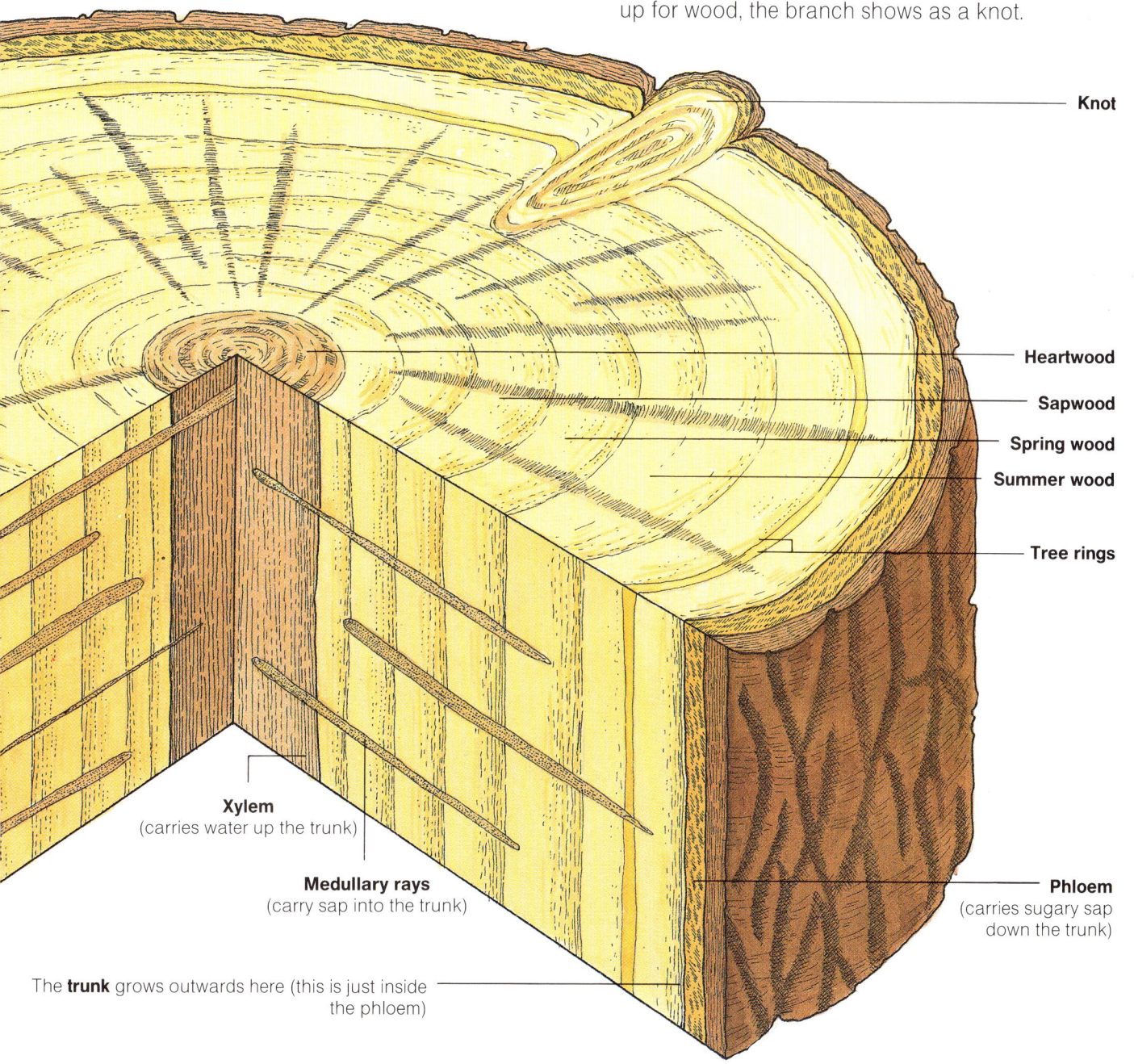

Knot

Heartwood

Sapwood

Spring wood

Summer wood

Tree rings

Xylem
(carries water up the trunk)

Medullary rays
(carry sap into the trunk)

The **trunk** grows outwards here (this is just inside the phloem)

Phloem
(carries sugary sap down the trunk)

How we use plants

Human beings have eaten food from plants for millions of years. The first tools that our ancestors made probably came from plants. Throughout history we have used plant products in many different ways – to build houses, carts and ships, and to make everything from clothing and medicines, to rope and paper. Today, we use plant products less, because **synthetic** man-made materials have replaced them. These synthetics include plastics, nylon and acrylic fabric.

The earliest aeroplanes were made of **sitka spruce**, a type of softwood that can be very strong but not heavy.

Bamboo is a grass with very thick, strong stems. It makes attractive furniture.

The black keys of a piano are made from a rare wood called **ebony**.

Most paper is made from wood, which is reduced to a pulp and then rolled out flat.

Raffia comes from the long leaves of the **raffia palm**.

Coconut matting comes from the rough outer coat of the coconut seed.

The thick bark of the **cork oak** gives us cork, which is unusual because it is so elastic – it can be squashed by pressing hard, but it bounces back into shape afterwards. This makes it useful for bottle-stoppers and floors.

Rope and sacks used to be made from the tough brown fibres of the **jute** plant. Most of it is now made from synthetic fibres.

Cotton is spun from fine fibres that are attached to the seeds of the **cotton** plant.

Linen, used for tablecloths and clothing, comes from strong fibres in the stem of the **flax** plant.

Rubber was once made from trees. When a cut is made in the trunk of the rubber tree, a thick, sticky liquid oozes out. Today, almost all rubber is synthetic.

Count the plants

Look for all the different plant products in the picture. Write down the names of the plants they come from. **How many different plants are there?** Clues: the piano frame is made of **walnut**, the table of **yellow pine**, and the chairs of **ash wood**. The picture frames are **mahogany**. The doors and windows are made of yellow pine. All the paper is made from **lodgepole pine**.

★ ANSWERS ★

Twenty-seven plants are represented here – nine trees (cork, oak, lodgepole pine, yellow pine, ash, walnut, mahogany, ebony, rubber and sitka spruce), two palms (coconut and raffia), one grass (bamboo); five fruits (banana, pineapple, grapefruit, orange and pear); three houseplants (fern, spider plant and geranium); one herb (parsley); plus three others (jute, cotton and flax). Did you also get the final three? Grapes (for the wine on the table), coffee (in the mug) and cut flowers (in the vase)!

Farms and gardens

At one time, human beings lived by hunting and gathering wild plant foods. About 12,000 years ago, people living in the Middle East found that if grass seeds were ground down between two stones, mixed with water and then cooked over a fire, they made a very good food – bread.

Instead of wandering about, as they had done before, they stayed in one place, cleared away other plants, and planted grass seeds. This is how farming began. They also found out that instead of hunting animals, they could breed them and keep them in one place.

CHANGING THE GRAIN

Once people began planting the grasses, they had become farmers. Each year they would save some of the best seed to sow next year. By choosing the best seed they were 'improving' the grasses. The plants became stronger as the years passed, and the seeds fatter. This process of choosing is called *selective breeding*.

Today, selective breeding is mostly carried out by scientists who understand what is happening inside the plant. They can make changes in a plant much more quickly than those early farmers, using new scientific methods.

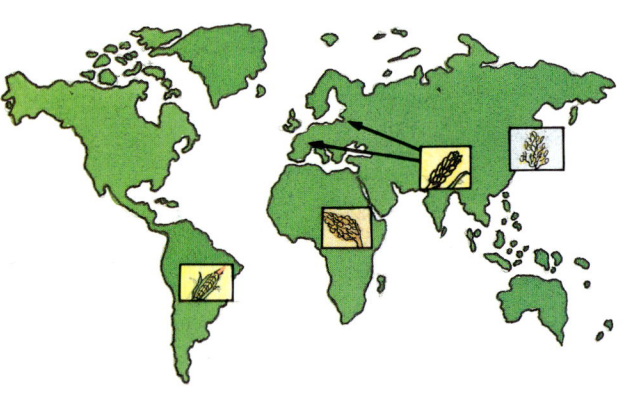

wheat

rice

maize

millet

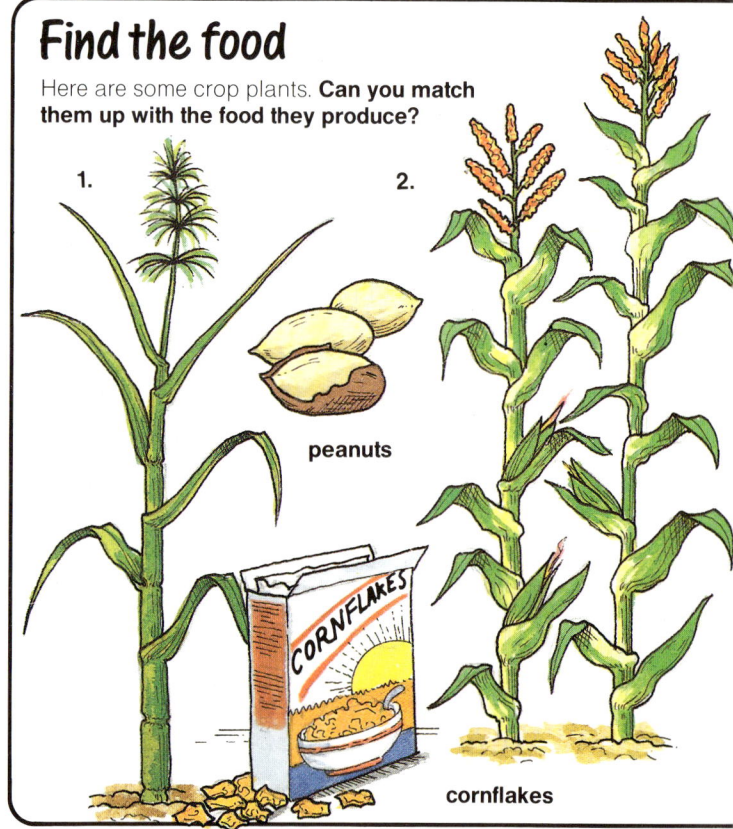

Find the food

Here are some crop plants. **Can you match them up with the food they produce?**

1.

2.

peanuts

cornflakes

CROPS AROUND THE WORLD

Wheat became the main food or *staple crop* in the Middle East. From there, it slowly spread to Europe, as farmers moved north and west. In China, they also made a grass into their staple crop – **rice**. In Central America, they chose another grass, which eventually gave **maize** (corn). In Africa, three grasses were turned into crops – two are known as **millet** and one as **sorghum**. These grass crops are all known as *cereals*.

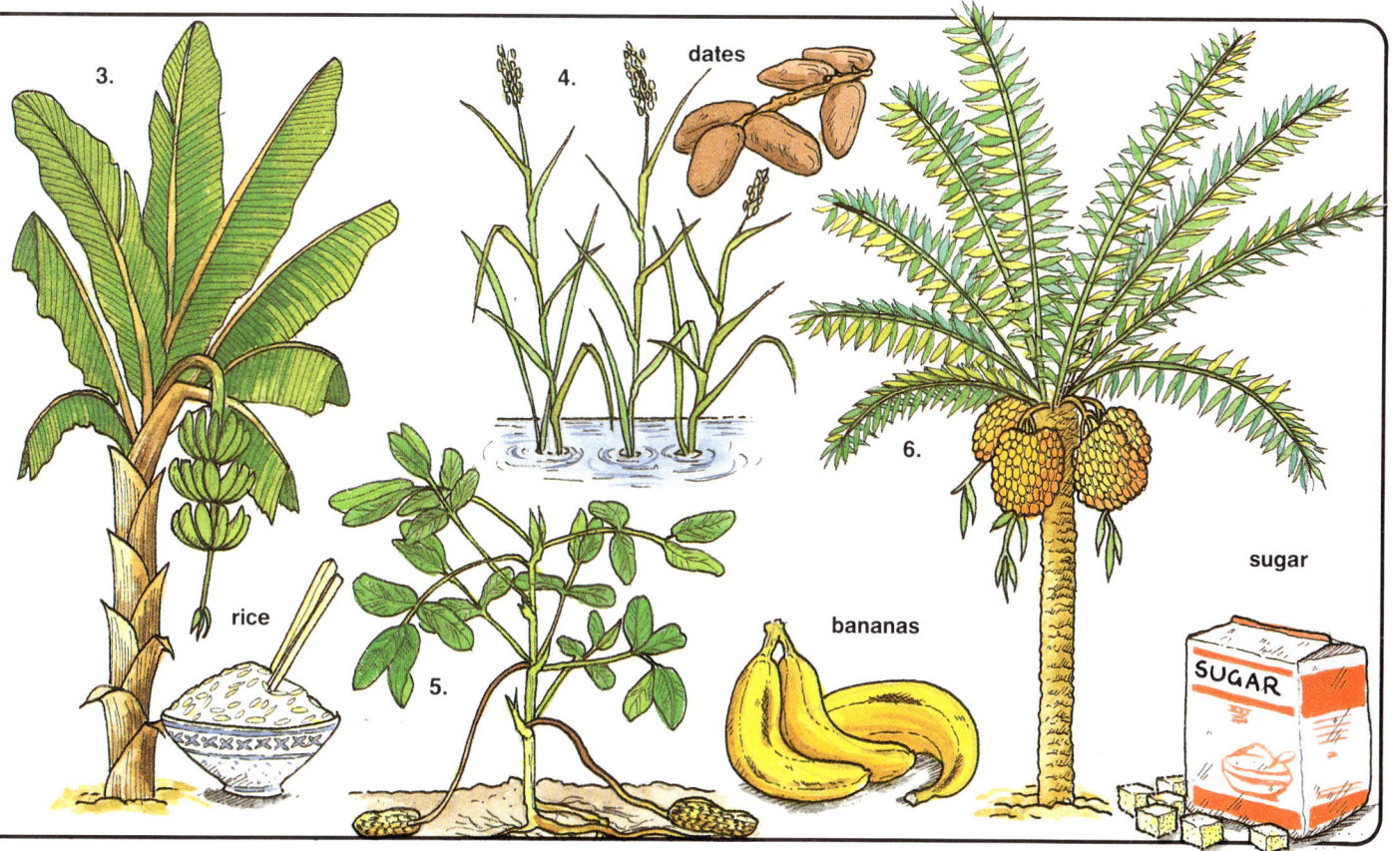

3.

dates

4.

rice

5.

bananas

6.

sugar

SUGAR

FARMING TODAY

To protect them from insects and diseases, crops are often sprayed with *pesticides*. Unfortunately, most of these chemicals are harmful to wildlife and people, and cause pollution.

Saving our plants

Can you imagine a world without plants? Everybody everywhere needs plants for food and oxygen. As plants give out oxygen, they also take in carbon dioxide. Our power plants, cars and heating systems all give out carbon dioxide, and we need plants to absorb it. If it stays in the air, it makes the earth warmer, because of what is known as the **greenhouse effect**. If this happens, many places that are now green could become dry, dusty deserts.

YESTERDAY'S RAINFORESTS

Rainforests have been called 'the lungs of the world' because they give out so much oxygen and absorb so much carbon dioxide. They have more plants and animals in them than any other place on earth. But today, they are being destroyed at an incredible pace, to make room for crops or for their timber. When the farmers leave, the forest may never grow back again.

LOSING THE SOIL

Trees and bushes form a natural barrier to the wind and rain. Their roots bind the soil together. In many countries where the forests have been cleared, the soil is now being washed away. Without the soil, plants cannot grow. Eventually only barren, rocky land, or in some places deserts, remain.

Start your own garden

Most garden shops now sell wildflower seeds. You can use these to grow a wildflower garden. Or you can collect seeds from the wild, when they ripen in late summer. Remember to take just a few seeds from each plant, do not use all of them. Put them in paper bags, not plastic, and keep them in the refrigerator until next spring. Sow them in seed trays, and keep them well watered. Plant them in a weed-free flower bed when they have four or six leaves. You will have to care for the seedlings until they are big enough to grow without protection. When the plants flower, watch for butterflies and other insects that come to visit them. And look on the leaves for caterpillars and other insects. By growing wildflowers, you are providing a picnic for many wild animals!

PLANTS AND THE LAW

Plants are protected by law in many countries, and you should not dig up any wild plant without asking the person who owns the land. Some rare plants have special protection. If you pick them, the flowers cannot produce seeds, so if they are annuals they will not appear next year.

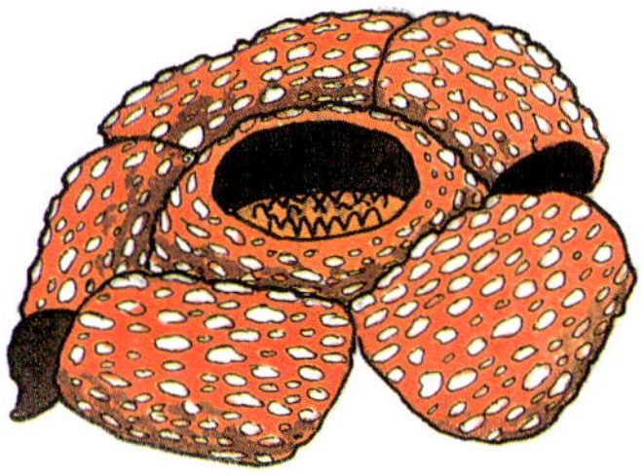

Fritillary

Calabrian primrose

Spring gentian

Rafflesia

New Zealand brush lily

Lady's slipper orchid

Quiz time

Here are some more plant teasers that you can solve by looking back through the book. If you can find the answers to these, you have made a great start exploring the world of plants.

You can find out more about the wonderful world of plants by reading books, watching nature programmes on television, growing plants in the garden or on a windowsill and keeping your eyes open wherever you go. Keep a record of everything you see.

PUZZLING PLANTS

Plants, like animals, have to 'behave' in ways that help them to survive. Here are seven plants doing rather strange things. **Can you explain what they're up to?**

The **waterlily** grows in water. The leaf stalks can grow to any length, from a few centimetres to over a metre.

The **coconut palm** grows on islands in the ocean, often on the shore. Its seed is contained in a large fruit – the coconut – which has its own supply of 'water' inside. The nut is covered by a very tough shell and a thick coat of hair.

Canadian pondweed is a flowering plant like the waterlily. Its flowers are tiny, but the stalk is very long.

Which group of plants?

Putting plants in the right group is important when beginning to explore plants. Try to put these four plants in the correct group.

1.

2.

3.

4.

Mangrove trees grow in swampy areas by the sea, where the tide goes in and out every day. Their seeds germinate before they leave the tree, producing a root that has a hard sharp point.

The **bee orchid** has flowers that look just like a particular type of bee – the female of the species. The flower even feels and smells like a bee. It is so lifelike that male bees try to mate with the flower.

Ivy-leaved toadflax grows on cliffs and walls. When the seeds are developing, the stalks that carry the seeds grow away from the light.

When the trunk or branch of a **pine tree** is cut, a thick liquid called resin oozes out. It is sticky and smells strongly. **What do you think it is for?**

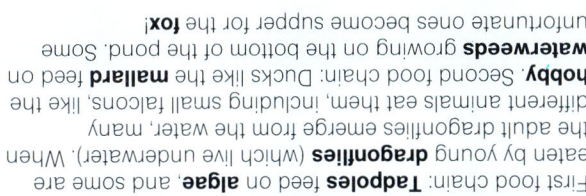

★ ANSWERS ★

WHICH GROUP OF PLANTS?

1. This is a **tree fern**. These unusually tall ferns grow mostly in tropical forests.

2. It is usually safe to call trees with cones conifers, but there is an important exception, and here it is! The **alder** is a flowering plant, but has small woody cones. Its leaves should have made you suspicious of course – no conifer has leaves like this.

3. This is a flowering plant – the largest flower in the world, known as **Rafflesia**. It is a parasite.

4. This is a flowering plant – like all grasses, it has very small flowers, without colour or scent, because it is pollinated by the wind.

PUZZLING PLANTS

By growing away from the light, the seed stalks of the **ivy-leaved toadflax** push the seeds into cracks in the cliff or wall. The plants that grow from those seeds can then get a good 'hold' on the cliff or wall.

Mangrove seeds could easily be swept away by the tide when they fall from the tree. The spear-like root sticks into the mud to prevent this happening.

Coconuts rely on the sea to carry their seeds from island to island. The hair helps the coconut to float and the thick shell keeps sea-water out. When the seed reaches an island, it needs to get its roots down, through the sand, before it can find fresh water. The 'water' inside the coconut helps it through this difficult time.

The **waterlily** is descended from land plants. It needs the kind of sunlight found at the surface, not light that has filtered through water. Its leaves are a good shape for floating on the surface. But the waterlily may find itself growing in a shallow pond or a deep lake. So its leaf stalks grow to whatever length is needed.

Canadian pondweed has gone one step further than the waterlily, because it has learned to use the light that filters down through water. But it still needs flying insects like bees to pollinate its flowers. So, however deep it is in the pond, it pushes its flowers up to the surface on long stalks. The **bee orchid** relies on the male bee to take its pollen from one flower to another. If the bee tries to mate with one bee orchid, then with another, the pollen will be transferred.

The **pine** resin engulfs insects and other small animals that try to feed on the tree's sap. Its smell comes from chemicals, some of which can kill insects.

MAKE YOUR OWN FOOD CHAIN

First food chain: **Tadpoles** feed on **algae**, and some are eaten by young **dragonflies** (which live underwater). When the adult dragonflies emerge from the water, many different animals eat them, including small falcons, like the **hobby**. Second food chain: Ducks like the **mallard** feed on **waterweeds** growing on the bottom of the pond. Some unfortunate ones become supper for the **fox**!

37

Index